One Size does not Fit All

beverly Naidus

Aigis Publications
Littleton, Colorado

One Size does not Fit All, first published by Aigis Publications, 1993
(an earlier artist's edition was self–published by the author as *The Fat Book*, 1991)

Cover Design by Jody Chapel, Cover to Cover Design

Printed on acid free paper with soy–based inks
Manufactured in the United States

Library of Congress Cataloging–in–Publication Data
Naidus, Beverly, 1953–
One size does not fit all / Beverly Naidus.
p. cm.
Originally published under title: The fat book, 1992.
Includes bibliographical references.
ISBN 1–883930–01–4 (alk. paper): $35.00. — ISBN 1–883930–00–6 (pbk.: alk. paper): $15.00
1. Overweight women—Mental health. 2. Self–acceptance. 3. Body image. I. Title
RC552.025N35 1993
158'.1'082—dc20 93–30780
CIP

Aigis Publications, 1449 W. Littleton Blvd., Suite 200, Littleton, CO 80120
(303)730-6232 tel., (303)798-6568 fax

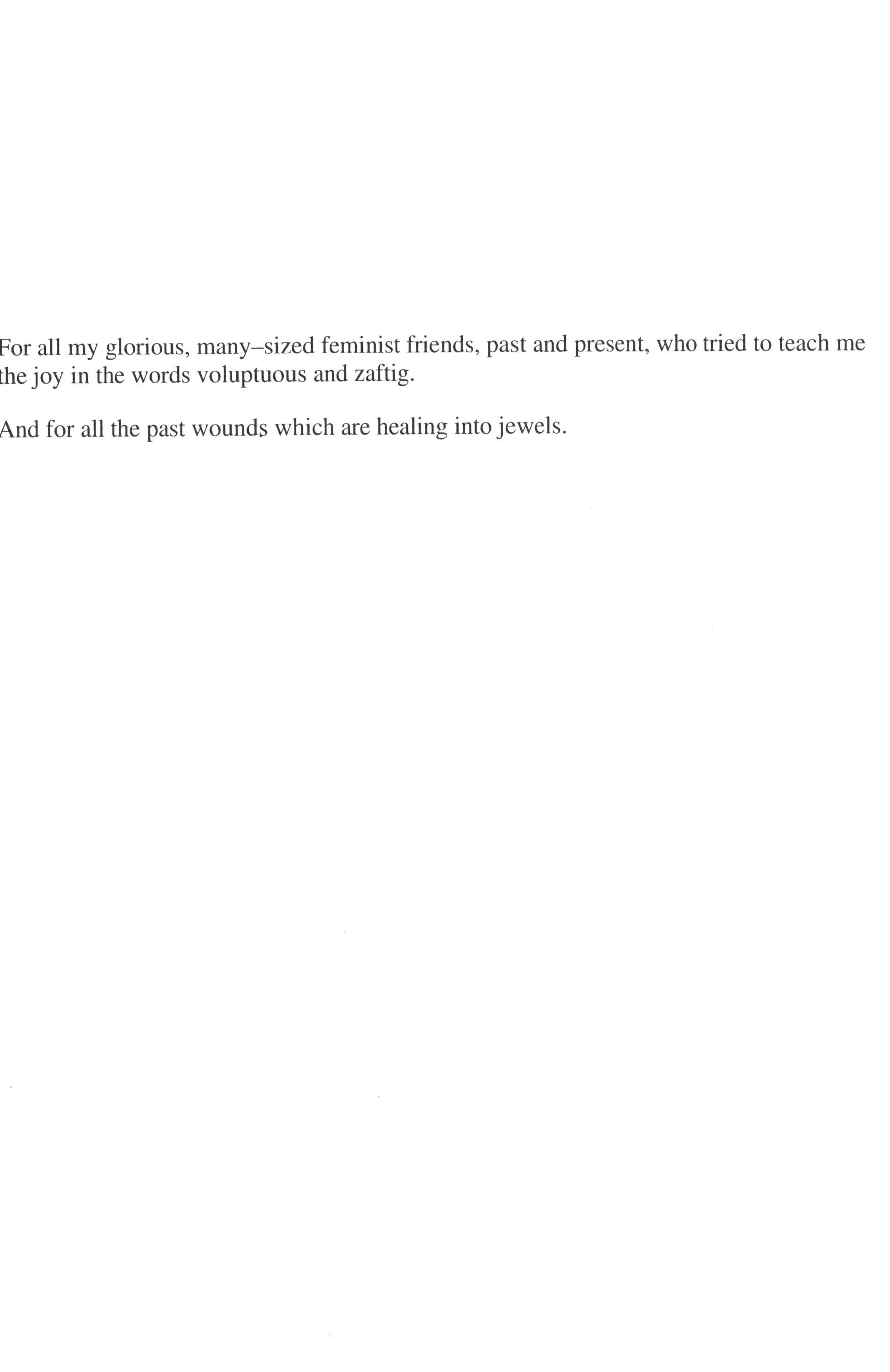

For all my glorious, many–sized feminist friends, past and present, who tried to teach me the joy in the words voluptuous and zaftig.

And for all the past wounds which are healing into jewels.

The world's problems weighed upon her, but first she'd have to lose some weight.

There was
always
something
wrong with
her body.

She was raised
to be ashamed
of her body

She could
never figure
out what size
she
was.

She appeared to be at ease in her body, but she couldn't find her center.

No one would have guessed her secret obsession with food...

Her mother
taught her, like
almost all mothers taught
their daughters, the painful
art of self-surveillance.

Comparing buttocks
and thighs,
wrinkles and sags,
she broke bodies
into pieces. Now
where could
she have
learned that?!!

when she ate
until she was
full she felt
guilty.

She felt
as if she
would
explode

She tried to pretend
she didn't feel self-conscious
while walking on the beach.

She wanted to occupy a lot of space.

She held her spare tire like a security blanket!

Trying on clothes was pure torture

She dressed to hide her body.

She kept
all the
now too
small
clothes
just in
case…

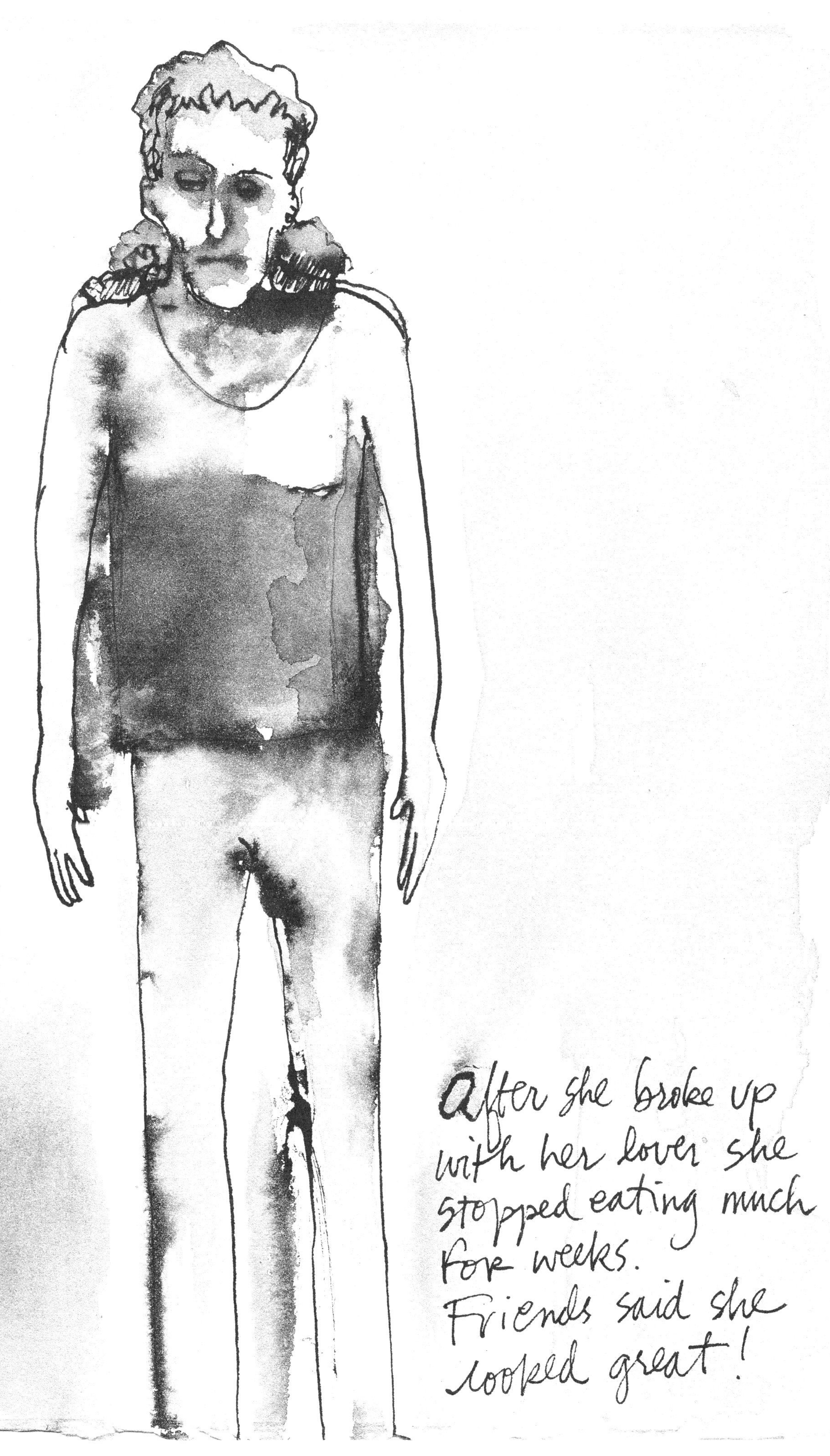
After she broke up
with her lover she
stopped eating much
for weeks.
Friends said she
looked great!

She prayed to be released from
her obsession with food.

If she didn't diet
she felt she would expand
infinitely

Her lover and her friends,
who enjoyed her unique beauty,
grew frustrated
with her endless
self-abuse.

She kept dreaming
she'd wake up
thin.

She was told
that her
double chin
was
grotesque.

No matter how many times she was told by friends and lovers, "You Look Great!"she never really believed it.

She said her sister was
going to pay for her
chin lift.

She was
told she'd
never marry
a lawyer
with an ass
like that.

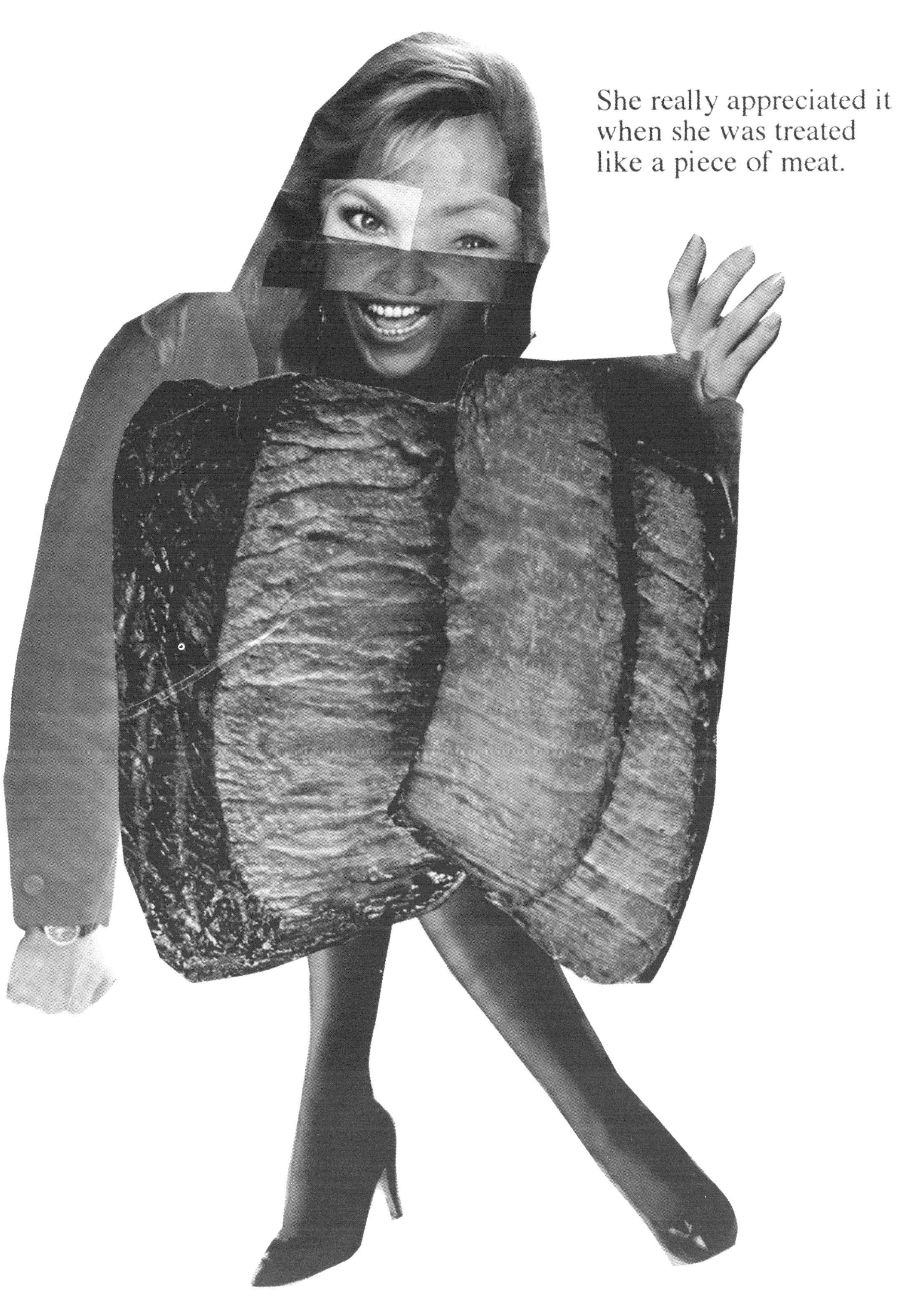
She really appreciated it
when she was treated
like a piece of meat.

Trips to the
supermarket
were fraught
with anxiety.

If she didn't exercise
everyday she
thought she'd blow
up like a balloon.

She looked forward to looking like everyone else.

Only in her
sleep could
she forget
about
her body

Having done every diet available,
she considered the possibility
of a lobotomy.

She felt
like her
body was
out of
control.

She wanted
to snip and
fuck all
over.

She tried a
daily affirmation
and forgiveness
diet,
but it
didn't work.

There was always something wrong with her body.

As she became more self-fulfilled in the outside world, the domain of her body became a war zone, with one army tirelessly at battle.

She was sick of being
told she was born in
the wrong century.

The exquisite, but rare
moments of external
approval had a
very limited
shelf life.

Being comfortable in her
body did not come easily.

She was told
that her
varicose veins
were disgusting.

She felt assaulted by the daily barrage of diet programs and products.
250 calories
500 calories
My waist had ballooned
Now it's back to 25 and
again. I love you for mal
beautiful again.
FREE-N-LEAN
FAT FREE
LOW CHOLES
1 oz. mixed nuts, 17 g fat
The Delicious, Nutr
LOSE WEIG
Fried shrimp with tartar sa
27 g fat
PREVENTION
WEIGHT-LOSS
FREE!
MAXIMUM STRENGTH
FAT FREE
WATCHERS
HAPPY HOLIDAYS!
No Dieting
No Pills
No Nervousness
No Frantic Exercising
Strange Formulas
Foods To Bu
Boiled shrimp with cocktail sauce, 3 g fat
30 pounds in 30 days? Right
Actually, I lost 33 pounds in
30 days. I still can't believe it.
Fettucine Alfredo, 28 g fat
370 calories
Lose Weight With Great Tas
Lose the fat.
YOU CAN LOSE
Steady Control
Appetite Suppressant
OPTIFAST CORE
CALORIE COUNTER
Strawberry sorbet, 0 g fat
Fettucine with marinara sauce, 10 g fat

She got fed up
with the
expression
"she let
herself go."

"No Fat Chicks"
bumperstickers
drove her nuts.

She had had it with face lifts.

Her boyfriend
suggested a breast
lift. She
suggested a
brain lift.

Peer pressure failed to bring
a razor to her left calf.

ADVERTISERS, DEPENDENT ON HER CONSUMPTION, WANTED HER COMPLETELY DISTRACTED BY THE GOAL OF SELF-PERFECTION

Her doctor told her she had a "weight problem" and recommended a thyroid test. She told him to shove it.

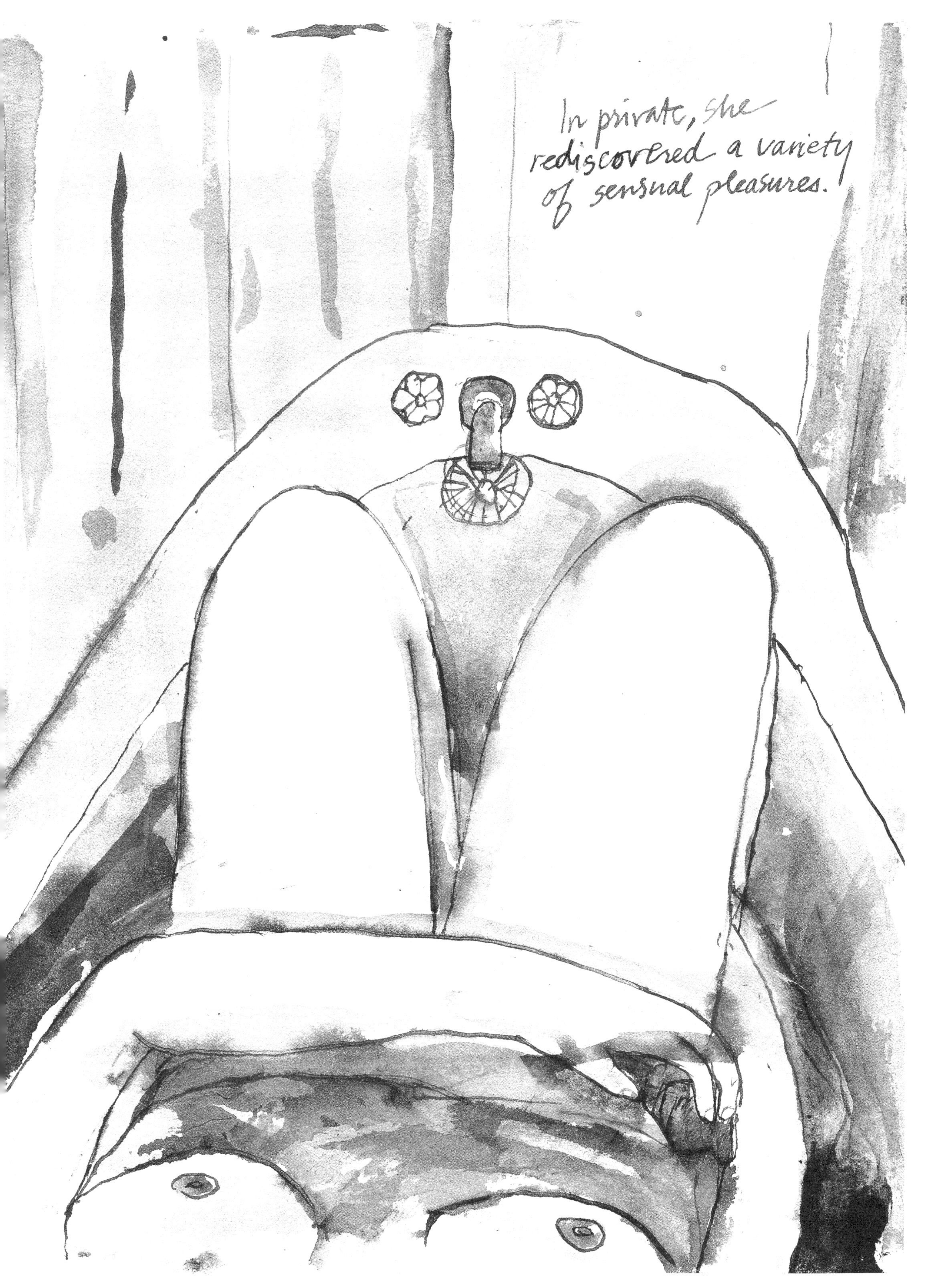
In private, she rediscovered a variety of sensual pleasures.

Her doctor told her she was quite large for a vegetarian and asked her if she snuck donuts in the closet. She asked him if he'd like to have his face rearranged.

She grew
weary of
obsessing
about
her body.

She grew impatient with the endless discussions of weight among her friends.

She learned
to just sit
and breathe.

She slowly learned to accept compliments gracefully.

She wondered where the concepts of "underweight" and "overweight" came from? And who was persecuting her with this idea of normalcy?

She tried to stop torturing herself with fashion pornography.

The external sources
of her oppression
began to
become apparent.

She swore off diets and scales
and joined a body image
support group.

She decided not to worry.

She got fed up with the fashion industry and developed her own sense of style.

Everytime she fell back into
worrying about her weight
she realized there was
something else more
profoundly
disturbing her.

She practiced loving herself
by enjoying the diversity
of body styles
she saw in the sauna.

She tried to
make friends
with her
mirror.

She discovered that food wasn't dangerous
and began to enjoy the
diversity of taste and textures.
She ate with relish until she was satisfied.

Internalizing goddess
imagery was only
moderately helpful.

She learned to accept the uniqueness of her body.

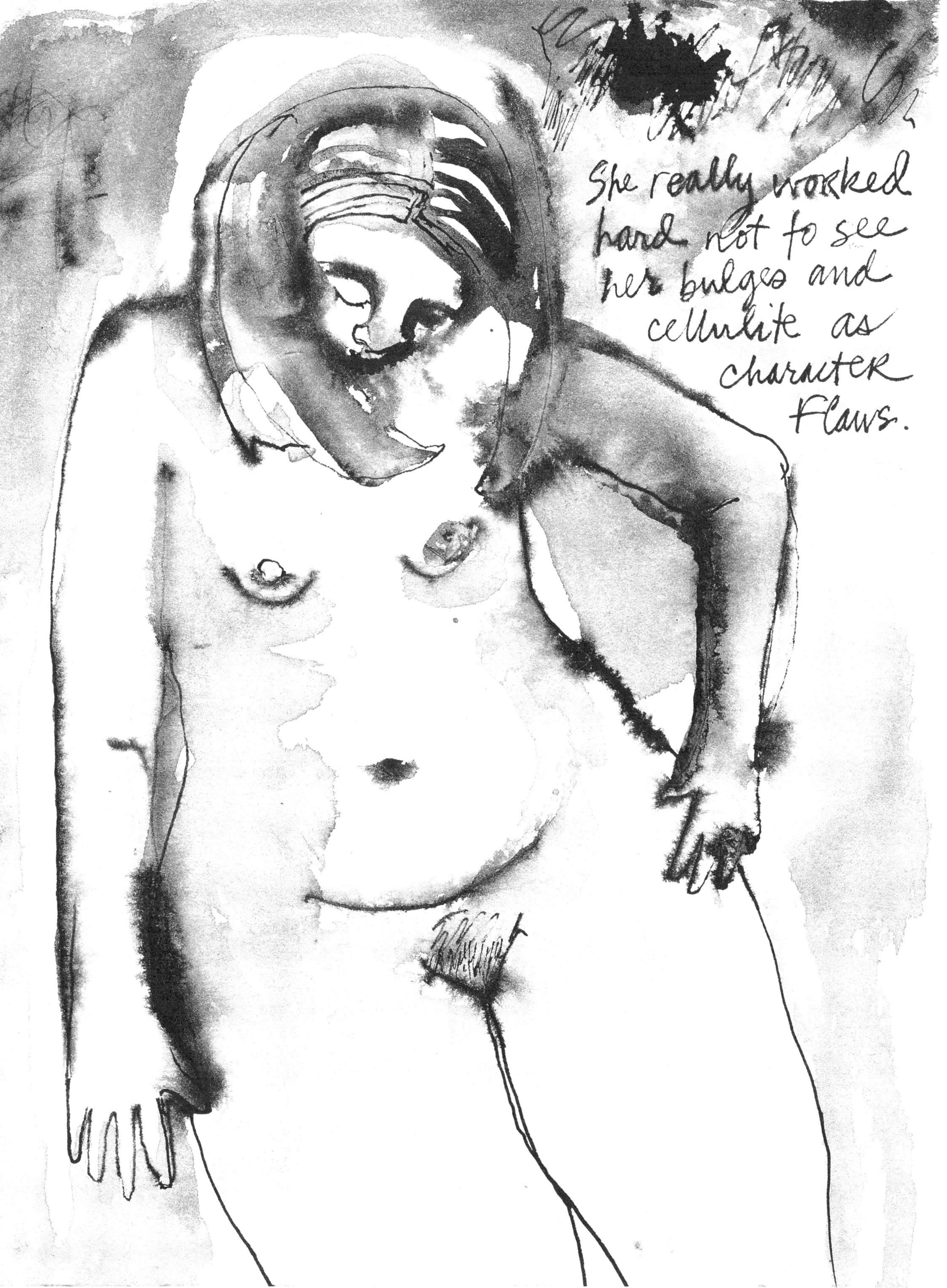
She really worked hard not to see her bulges and cellulite as character flaws.

She learned that exercise
could be about strength, power, and fun,
rather than about boredom
and self-abuse.

She tried to
make friends
with Food.

She took control of
her boundaries.

She began
to feel her
body below
the neck.

She recognized that her healing would be a life long process with many ups and downs.

Of course, there were still days when looking in the mirror cancelled out all the progress she'd made.

elf-hate still haunted her
om time to time,
ut she learned to
ve with it.

She moved
with
great
grace.

No one could make her feel bad about her body again.

She learned
to love
her
body

She celebrated
her health
and vitality.

She danced in honor of her body that had taken her everywhere she needed to go all these years.

One Size does not Fit All (previously known as The Fat Book)

In the summer of 1987 I was spending time with a writer friend back East, trying to process my first year in Southern California through my art. I cautiously began to do sketches and watercolors dealing with obsessions about body image. It was a very tentative beginning to this series. I was both embarrassed and self–critical about having such an issue enter the realm of my artmaking. It seemed so self–indulgent and trivial compared to all of the deep suffering and injustice in the world. I hid the work away and went back to more "serious" art projects.

Up until that time I had been reading everything I could get my hands on regarding women and their discontent with their bodies. In the early eighties I had read *Fat Is a Feminist Issue* by Susie Orbach. It answered a few questions, but it still seemed to be based on the idea that if you worked out all your issues around food, you would miraculously lose weight. I was much more inspired in late 1987 when I found Kim Chernin's *The Hungry Self* and *The Obsession: The Tyranny of Slenderness.* With more enthusiasm I began to paint a series about "body hate," which included some of my stories and others I heard from my friends. In 1990, I found the book *Shadow on a Tightrope: Writings by Women on Fat Oppression*, and I began to do some real healing on the issue of fat.

What acted as the midwife for the birth of this book was an experience I had at the Institute for Social Ecology in Plainfield, Vermont. In the summer of 1991, I was asked there to lead a workshop on "Activist Art." I was able to sit in on an Ecofeminism class (taught by Chaia Heller) and participate in a body image workshop (led by Alexa Berton) with 15 young women. These were all attractive, highly intelligent women in their twenties. We went around in a circle naming the things we most liked and disliked about our bodies. The lists of dislikes were very long. It was painful to listen to the litanies of self–hate: stories about mothers torturing daughters with diet programs and pills, and teenagers teaching each other to throw up. And when it came to the list of likes they found little to say: "my wrists," "my ears," "my nose...." As the designated, thirtysomething sage in the group, I had to admit I was horrified by how damaged these women were.

In the Ecofeminism class I learned how deeply internalized body hate is among women in our culture, no matter what age, what cultural background, what class, what race, or what size. The fashion industry and the media have done an enormous amount of damage, and often our families, friends, and mates have reinforced it. I began to recognize the connection between self–esteem issues and the dysfunction of the society as a whole. I saw how necessary it is to develop support groups which critique the status quo. In such groups we can begin to question why so much emphasis is placed on the body (our only domain of "control" in a society where we have been deeply disempowered), and we can develop the tools to heal ourselves. It is a long process, but so much creative energy can be unleashed when we take those first steps to enjoy our uniqueness.

After my experience at the Institute, I understood how important it was to get this work out (although there was still a part of me that felt I needed to lose weight first (really!) before I could go public with this work). My sense of urgency overrode my inhibitions as I saw that the obsession with body size continued to sap my energy and the energy of all my talented, intelligent, strong, attractive women friends. I decided it had to be in the form of a bookwork so it could be distributed widely and many people could see it.

The original *The Fat Book* was reviewed by Judith Hoffberg in *Umbrella Magazine* (Fall '92): "...Rather than a heavy textbook or moralistic or philosophical tome, this visual book serves as a catalyst for discussion, projection, and action for many women all over the nation. A must!" Over 150 copies of the original laser–copied, 60–paged, artist's edition sold through word of mouth, and at a few galleries and bookstores. I received a great deal of encouragement from the bookwork's audience: therapists have used it with their clients, women have used it for their self–healing and have shared it with the women in their lives, and men have also been enthusiastic about using and sharing it. Some of the new images in this revised edition were influenced by my audience and by my reading of Naomi Wolf's recent book, *The Beauty Myth*, a powerful and much needed addition to the discussion of this subject.

I owe a great deal to the work being done by the courageous members of the Fat Liberation Movement. Their writings and research have been very important to my understanding of size oppression. Many articles in *Shadow on a Tightrope* and Joan Drury's essay *Physicalism* are excellent contributions on that topic. As was pointed out to me by Mimi Orner of the Fat Chance Theater in Madison, Wisconsin and others, "problematic relationships with food" should not necessarily be linked with fat. Such a linkage is a stereotype and part of the negative mythology created about fat people.

I would like this bookwork to be used as a tool for women and men* (in support–group contexts or individually) who are trying to heal themselves in relation to their body hate. Hopefully, people will be inspired to make their own drawings and write their own stories and share them with others.

This bookwork could not exist without the support and love of my soulmate, collaborator, and husband, Bob Spivey. Other people who provided inspiration, encouragement, and/or the space for this work to happen have been the ecofeminists of the Institute for Social Ecology, friends from the Ojai Foundation, Joseph Heflin, Alexa Berton, and Signe Timm. I received very helpful feedback and support from Paula Emery, Lloyd Strecker, Morgan Alexander, Kate Mack, Stephen Foster, Meredith Little, Lynne Dahlgren, Wendy L'Homme, Maggie Tennesen, Vivienne Stein, Mary Cecile Gee, and Annie Appel. For design assistance on the advance review copies and for all of his suggestions, I want to thank Tim Drewitt of Turnaround Graphics. I am very grateful to all those (too numerous to name) who made this work possible. The major part of this bookwork was produced in my former studio at Angel's Gate Cultural Center in San Pedro, CA while on a professional leave of absence from my teaching position at California State University—Long Beach. The final revisions occurred in my new studio in Venice, CA. And finally, without the enthusiastic support of Pavlos Stavropoulos and Aigis Publications, this book would not be in front of you now.

Some of the original paintings, drawings, and/or photocollages in this series were exhibited at the South Bay Contemporary Museum in Torrance, CA; the House of Envy Beauty Salon in Long Beach, CA; BC Space in Laguna Beach, CA; a group show curated by Sheila Pinkel entitled "Vantage Points" at California Polytechnic, Pomona, CA; a "Works on Paper" show at California State University—Long Beach; a group show at UCLA's student union gallery; at Highways performance space gallery in Santa Monica, CA; and at Side Street Projects in Santa Monica, CA. An installation concerning the same issues as the book was shown at the Paseo Nuevo mall in Santa Barbara, CA in the fall of 1993, sponsored by the Santa Barbara Contemporary Arts Forum in a show entitled "Back Talk: Women's Voices in the Nineties," curated by Marilu Knode and Erica Daborn.

*How men might use this book:

Although I have not illustrated the stories of men in this bookwork, it has been made clear to me that *One Size Does Not Fit All* has a large male audience. It can be used by individual men to work on their own issues regarding body image (eating disorders among the male population have increased in recent years, and certain obsessions about body size and shape have always existed for some men). Obviously, it would make sense for a man working through such issues to make his own images and text and share them with others. It would perhaps take some courage to do that, but it would be enormously healing, not only for himself, but for others with similar issues.

The more sizable (bad pun) male audience for this bookwork is the one living with or associating with women who are obsessed with their bodies. Some men are very concerned about the damaged and/or hurting women around them and want to be effective assistants in the healing process. While this bookwork may not address all the issues your friend, family member, or mate is going through, it may put her on the right path. But that is assuming she is ready to look at it. There are a few women who will look at this book and say, "this might be fine for someone else, but I won't be happy with myself until I lose some weight." It is difficult to be the lone voice in the wilderness saying, "I love you just the way you are" when all the advertising and sometimes peer and family pressure is saying the opposite. We women sometimes have a way of turning such compliments around so that they resonate like insults. And, in such cases, the most well–intentioned man can't win. My hope is that reading some of the books suggested in my bibliography together, looking at the images in this bookwork, and sharing insights through words, images, songs, video, etc., might be good first steps. Patience is the key. It is a life–long process. Recognizing the external causes of the oppression will move women to a higher political consciousness, and the energy unleashed by that cannot help but be transformative.

Bibliographical information:

These books had a direct influence on the content of this bookwork:

Chernin, Kim. *The Obsession: Reflections on the Tyranny of Slenderness.* NY: Harper and Row, 1981.

___________. *The Hungry Self: Women, Eating, and Identity.* London: Virago Press, 1986.

Drury, Joan. *Physicalism.* Minneapolis: Spinsters Ink, 1992.

Orbach, Susie. *Fat Is a Feminist Issue.* NY: Berkley Books, 1979.

Schoenfielder, Lisa and Barb Wieser, eds. *Shadow on a Tightrope, Writings by Women on Fat Oppression.* San Francisco: Aunt Lute Books, 1983.

Wolf, Naomi. *The Beauty Myth: How Images of Beauty Are Used Against Women.* NY: Doubleday, 1991.

For more research on this subject:

Jacobus, Mary, Evelyn Fo Keller and Sally Shuttleworth, eds. *Body/Politics: Women and the Discourses of Science.* NY: Routledge, 1990.

Millman, Marcia. *Such a Pretty Face.* NY: W.W. Norton, 1980.

Roth, Geneen. *Feeding the Hungry Heart.* NY: Penguin, 1982.

Seid, Roberta Pollack. *Never Too Thin: Why Women Are at War with Their Bodies.* NY: Prentice–Hall, 1989.

Szekeley, Eva. *Never Too Thin.* Toronto: The Women's Press, 1988. I recently discovered this excellent analysis of the complex social issues surrounding women's body hate.

Adbusters: Journal of the Mental Environment, The Media Foundation, 1243 West 7th Avenue, Vancouver, B.C. V6H 1B7, Canada, (800) 663–1243. This in an excellent journal on media literacy with satirical critiques of fashion pornography.

Radiance Magazine, P.O. Box 30246, Oakland, CA 94604, (510) 482–0680. Interestingly enough, this magazine could not be found in any alternative bookstore in the Los Angeles area. In its ninth year, this publication is devoted to the positive health and well–being of women all sizes of large.

Organizations:

National Association to Advance Fat Acceptance (NAAFA)
P.O. Box 43
Bellerose, NY 11426

NAAFA
P.O. Box 188620
Sacramento, CA 95818
(916) 443–0303

Start your own support group. Put up a flier at the library, bookstore, food co–op, health food store, health club, day care center, school, or at work. Share your stories about your likes and dislikes about your bodies. Write them down, act them out, dance them, sing them, or draw them. Talk about what is necessary to create a positive self–image. Read some of the books listed here and discuss them. Create strategies for educating others and devise some fun, provocative public actions and/or dialogues.

Contacting the author:

Beverly Naidus is available for book signings, workshops, and lectures. Exhibits of her art can also be arranged. To inquire about any of the above, or if you want to contact the author please write to:

Beverly Naidus
c\o Aigis Publications
1449 West Littleton Blvd., Suite 200
Littleton, CO 80120

To order additional copies, please send a check or money order payable to Aigis Publications at the above address for $15.00 plus $2.50 (shipping and handling) per copy ordered ($5.50 for airmail).